VIVA!
LATINO CELEBRATIONS

CELEBRATING HISPANIC HERITAGE MONTH!

MARISA ORGULLO

PowerKiDS press
New York

Published in 2019 by The Rosen Publishing Group, Inc.
29 East 21st Street, New York, NY 10010

Copyright © 2019 by The Rosen Publishing Group, Inc.

All rights reserved. No part of this book may be reproduced in any form without permission in writing from the publisher, except by a reviewer.

First Edition

Editor: Brianna Battista
Book Design: Reann Nye

Photo Credits: Cover, p. 1 (child) Robert Fried/Alamy Stock Photos; cover (background) Richard Levine/Alamy Stock Photos; p. 5 Corbis/Corbis/Getty Images; p. 7 Agencia Makro/LatinContent Editorial/Getty Images; p. 9 Diego Cervo/Shutterstock.com; p. 11 ESB Professional/Shutterstock.com; p. 13 TIM SLOAN/AFP/Getty Images; p. 15 Larry Busacca/Getty Images Entertainment/Getty Images; p. 17 Tita.ti/Shutterstock.com; p. 19 Fotoholica Press/ LightRocket/Getty Images; p. 21 Anton_Ivanov/Shutterstock.com; p. 22 Elpisterra/Shutterstock.com.

Cataloging-in-Publishing Data

Names: Orgullo, Marisa.
Title: Celebrating Hispanic heritage month! / Marisa Orgullo.
Description: New York : PowerKids Press, 2019. | Series: Viva! Latino celebrations | Includes glossary and index.
Identifiers: ISBN 9781538342169 (pbk.) | ISBN 9781538342183 (library bound) | ISBN 9781538342176 (6 pack)
Subjects: LCSH: Hispanic Heritage Month–Juvenile literature.
Classification: LCC E184.S75 O74 2019 | DDC 973'.0468-dc23

CPSIA Compliance Information: Batch Batch #CWPK19: For Further Information contact Rosen Publishing, New York, New York at 1-800-237-9932

CONTENTS

Cultural Pride 4

Hispanic Heroes 12

Marking Día de la Raza 18

Glossary 23

Index 24

Websites 24

Cultural Pride

Hispanic **Heritage** Month is a time for all Americans to **celebrate** Hispanic culture. Culture is the way people live. Hispanic people mark this festival by honoring special traditions from their background. Traditions are ways of doing things that have been passed down over time. Remembering traditions helps people stay connected to their family's **roots** and the countries they came from.

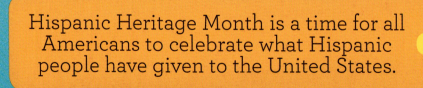

Hispanic Heritage Month is a time for all Americans to celebrate what Hispanic people have given to the United States.

Hispanic Heritage Month takes place in the United States from September 15 to October 15. These dates were chosen because autumn is a time when several Latin American countries celebrate their **independence** from Spain. Some of these nations are Costa Rica, El Salvador, Guatemala, Honduras, Nicaragua, Mexico, and Chile. In 1988, the U.S. government made it a time for the country to honor all Hispanic Americans.

These dancers are celebrating the day Chile marks its independence from Spain.

There are many Hispanic people living in the United States. Each family has its own story of what brought them here. Many live in places that were once part of Mexico. Others came from Central America, Mexico, or the Caribbean. Some were in search of better lives. They wanted to find safety or **freedom**.

Some Hispanic parents chose to come to America in search of better schools for their children.

The number of Hispanic families in the United States is growing higher each year. Today, 17.8 percent of people in the United States are Hispanic. That's more than one in every six Americans! Many Hispanic people live in the Southwest and in large midwestern and northeastern cities. Like other Americans, Hispanic people have many types of jobs. They are doctors, chefs, businesspeople, and reporters.

Some Hispanic people work in the United States as teachers.

Hispanic Heroes

Hispanic people have done amazing things for the United States! From the 1950s to the 1980s, a Mexican American named Cesar Chavez helped gain rights, such as fair pay and safe places to work, for farm workers. The first Hispanic U.S. **Supreme Court** justice is Sonia Sotomayor. Her family is from Puerto Rico.

Sonia Sotomayor became the first Latina Supreme Court justice in 2009.

Did you know that many sports players and actors are Hispanic? Tony Romo was a quarterback for the Dallas Cowboys. He was one of the first Hispanic people to lead an NFL football team. Selena Gomez is a Mexican and Italian American actress and pop star. You may have heard her songs on the radio. She has sold over 7 **million** albums.

Selena Gomez started out acting in the kids' television show *Barney and Friends*. She was only nine years old!

15

Hispanic Americans have given a lot to the art, music, and dance communities in the United States. Hispanic artists paint, draw, and take pictures. Salsa, a type of dance and music, has roots in the Caribbean. The tango, another type of dance, came out of Argentina. Hispanic culture has had a huge effect on the American arts.

An Argentinian man and woman dance the tango.

Marking Día de la Raza

Día de la Raza (DEE-ah DAY LAH RAH-sah), or Day of the Race, takes place on October 12. This day marks Christopher Columbus's arrival in the Americas. In the years that followed, Europeans killed many native people and wiped out many cultures. On Día de la Raza, people remember and celebrate the parts of native culture that survived.

Many people celebrate Día de la Raza by honoring their culture, such as this woman wearing traditional clothing from Peru.

There are many ways to learn about Hispanic culture. You can visit a museum and see Hispanic art, listen to music, learn a dance, or watch a movie. You could even learn some of the Spanish language! There are many fun ways to learn about Hispanic culture all year long.

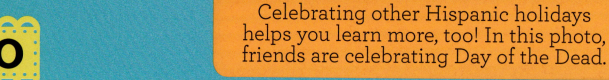

Celebrating other Hispanic holidays helps you learn more, too! In this photo, friends are celebrating Day of the Dead.

Hispanic Americans have played an important part in U.S. history. Our country is better because Hispanic American families have shared so much from their rich heritage. The culture is worth celebrating, during Hispanic Heritage Month and all year long.

GLOSSARY

celebrate: To honor an important moment by doing special things.

freedom: The power to do what you want to do.

heritage: The cultural traditions passed from parent to child.

independence: Freedom from the control or support of other people.

million: The number 1,000,000.

Supreme Court: The highest court in the United States.

roots: The family history of a person or a group of people.

INDEX

A
Argentina, 16

C
Caribbean, 8, 16
Central America, 8
Chavez, Cesar, 12
Chile, 6
Columbus, Christopher, 18
Costa Rica, 6
culture, 4, 16, 18, 20, 22

D
Día de la Raza, 18

E
El Salvador, 6

G
Gomez, Selena, 14
Guatemala, 6

H
Honduras, 6

M
Mexico, 6, 8

N
Nicaragua, 6

O
October, 6, 18

P
Peru, 18

R
Romo, Tony, 14

S
September, 6
Sotomayor, Sonia, 12
Spain, 6
Supreme Court, 12

U
United States, 4, 6, 8, 10, 12

WEBSITES

Due to the changing nature of Internet links, PowerKids Press has developed an online list of websites related to the subject of this book. This site is updated regularly. Please use this link to access the list: www.powerkidslinks.com/lcila/heritage